50 Cozy Breakfast Ideas for Winter Mornings

By: Kelly Johnson

Table of Contents

- Pumpkin Spice Oatmeal
- Apple Cinnamon Overnight Oats
- Savory Breakfast Bowl with Eggs and Spinach
- Hot Chocolate Smoothie Bowl
- Chai Spiced Chia Pudding
- Cinnamon Roll Pancakes
- Cheesy Egg and Potato Skillet
- Maple Pecan Granola with Yogurt
- Gingerbread Waffles
- Coconut Milk Rice Pudding
- Sweet Potato Hash with Eggs
- Winter Fruit Salad with Honey
- Nutty Quinoa Porridge
- Creamy Avocado Toast with Poached Eggs
- Blueberry Muffin Smoothie
- Baked Apple Cinnamon French Toast
- Creamy Tomato Soup with Grilled Cheese Croutons
- Banana Nut Overnight Oats
- Spiced Pear and Oatmeal Bowl
- Eggnog Pancakes
- Pineapple Coconut Smoothie
- Cranberry Almond Porridge
- Zucchini and Cheese Frittata
- Mushroom and Spinach Quiche
- Hazelnut Chocolate Spread on Toast
- Lemon Poppy Seed Muffins
- Warm Quinoa Bowl with Apples and Cinnamon
- Baked Eggs in Tomato Sauce
- Cocoa Oatmeal with Banana
- Honey Almond Butter Toast
- Sourdough Bread Pudding

- Maple Syrup Sweet Potato Pancakes
- Warm Cinnamon Apples with Yogurt
- Savory Oatmeal with Mushrooms and Cheese
- Homemade Breakfast Burritos
- Creamy Polenta with Sausage and Egg
- Chocolate Chip Banana Bread
- Strawberry and Cream Cheese Stuffed French Toast
- Spicy Sausage and Egg Breakfast Wrap
- Butternut Squash Soup with Toasted Seeds
- Cinnamon Sugar Donuts
- Rice Pudding with Cardamom
- Berry Smoothie Bowl with Granola
- Oven-Baked Omelet with Veggies
- Baked Oatmeal with Apples and Raisins
- Chocolate Hazelnut Overnight Oats
- Savory Breakfast Polenta
- Ricotta and Berry Toast
- Cinnamon Apple Pancakes
- Winter Root Vegetable Hash

Pumpkin Spice Oatmeal

Ingredients:

- 1 cup rolled oats
- 2 cups milk or almond milk
- 1/2 cup pumpkin puree
- 1 teaspoon pumpkin pie spice
- 2 tablespoons maple syrup (or honey)
- Pinch of salt
- Optional toppings: chopped nuts, dried cranberries, or whipped cream

Instructions:

1. In a saucepan, combine oats, milk, pumpkin puree, pumpkin pie spice, maple syrup, and salt.
2. Cook over medium heat, stirring occasionally, until the oatmeal thickens (about 5-7 minutes).
3. Serve hot, topped with your favorite toppings.

Apple Cinnamon Overnight Oats

Ingredients:

- 1 cup rolled oats
- 1 cup milk or almond milk
- 1 apple, diced
- 1 teaspoon cinnamon
- 1 tablespoon maple syrup (or honey)
- 1/4 cup Greek yogurt (optional)

Instructions:

1. In a jar or bowl, combine oats, milk, diced apple, cinnamon, maple syrup, and Greek yogurt.
2. Stir well, cover, and refrigerate overnight.
3. In the morning, stir again and enjoy cold or warmed.

Savory Breakfast Bowl with Eggs and Spinach

Ingredients:

- 2 eggs
- 2 cups fresh spinach
- 1/4 cup cherry tomatoes, halved
- 1/4 avocado, sliced
- Salt and pepper to taste
- Olive oil for cooking

Instructions:

1. In a skillet, heat olive oil over medium heat. Add spinach and cherry tomatoes, cooking until spinach is wilted.
2. In a separate pan, cook the eggs to your liking (scrambled, fried, or poached).
3. Assemble the bowl with spinach, tomatoes, eggs, and avocado slices. Season with salt and pepper.

Hot Chocolate Smoothie Bowl

Ingredients:

- 1 banana, frozen
- 1 cup almond milk (or milk of choice)
- 2 tablespoons cocoa powder
- 1 tablespoon maple syrup (or honey)
- Optional toppings: whipped cream, chocolate shavings, berries, or nuts

Instructions:

1. In a blender, combine the frozen banana, almond milk, cocoa powder, and maple syrup. Blend until smooth.
2. Pour into a bowl and top with your favorite toppings.

Chai Spiced Chia Pudding

Ingredients:

- 1/4 cup chia seeds
- 1 cup almond milk (or milk of choice)
- 1 tablespoon maple syrup (or honey)
- 1 teaspoon chai spice (or a mix of cinnamon, cardamom, and ginger)

Instructions:

1. In a bowl or jar, combine chia seeds, almond milk, maple syrup, and chai spice.
2. Stir well and refrigerate for at least 4 hours or overnight until it thickens.
3. Serve chilled, topped with fruit or nuts.

Cinnamon Roll Pancakes

Ingredients:

- 1 cup pancake mix
- 1 tablespoon cinnamon
- 1 tablespoon brown sugar
- 1/2 cup milk
- 1 egg
- Icing (optional): powdered sugar, milk, and vanilla extract for drizzling

Instructions:

1. In a bowl, combine pancake mix, cinnamon, brown sugar, milk, and egg until smooth.
2. Heat a non-stick skillet over medium heat and pour batter in circles to form pancakes.
3. Cook until bubbles form on the surface, then flip and cook until golden. Drizzle with icing if desired.

Cheesy Egg and Potato Skillet

Ingredients:

- 2 medium potatoes, diced
- 4 eggs
- 1/2 cup shredded cheese (cheddar or your choice)
- 1/4 onion, chopped
- Olive oil for cooking
- Salt and pepper to taste

Instructions:

1. In a skillet, heat olive oil over medium heat. Add diced potatoes and onions, cooking until potatoes are tender (about 10-12 minutes).
2. Make wells in the potatoes and crack an egg into each well. Cover and cook until the eggs are set.
3. Sprinkle cheese on top and cover until melted. Season with salt and pepper before serving.

Enjoy these delicious and hearty breakfast recipes!

Maple Pecan Granola with Yogurt

Ingredients:

- 2 cups rolled oats
- 1 cup pecans, chopped
- 1/2 cup maple syrup
- 1/4 cup coconut oil, melted
- 1 teaspoon vanilla extract
- 1/2 teaspoon salt
- Yogurt (Greek or your choice) for serving
- Optional toppings: fresh fruit, honey, or additional nuts

Instructions:

1. Preheat the oven to 350°F (175°C). Line a baking sheet with parchment paper.
2. In a large bowl, combine oats, pecans, maple syrup, melted coconut oil, vanilla extract, and salt. Mix until evenly coated.
3. Spread the granola mixture on the prepared baking sheet in an even layer. Bake for 20-25 minutes, stirring halfway, until golden brown.
4. Let cool and serve with yogurt and your choice of toppings.

Gingerbread Waffles

Ingredients:

- 1 1/2 cups all-purpose flour
- 1 tablespoon baking powder
- 1 teaspoon ground ginger
- 1 teaspoon ground cinnamon
- 1/2 teaspoon ground nutmeg
- 1/4 teaspoon ground cloves
- 1/4 teaspoon salt
- 2 tablespoons brown sugar
- 1 cup milk
- 1/4 cup vegetable oil
- 1 large egg
- Optional toppings: maple syrup, whipped cream, or pecans

Instructions:

1. Preheat your waffle maker according to the manufacturer's instructions.
2. In a large bowl, whisk together flour, baking powder, spices, salt, and brown sugar.
3. In another bowl, mix milk, vegetable oil, and egg. Combine wet and dry ingredients until just mixed.
4. Pour the batter into the preheated waffle maker and cook according to the manufacturer's instructions. Serve warm with desired toppings.

Coconut Milk Rice Pudding

Ingredients:

- 1 cup Arborio rice
- 4 cups coconut milk
- 1/2 cup sugar
- 1 teaspoon vanilla extract
- Pinch of salt
- Optional toppings: toasted coconut, fruit, or nuts

Instructions:

1. In a large saucepan, combine rice, coconut milk, sugar, vanilla extract, and salt. Bring to a boil over medium heat.
2. Reduce the heat to low and simmer, stirring frequently, until the rice is tender and the mixture thickens (about 30-40 minutes).
3. Remove from heat and let cool slightly. Serve warm or chilled, topped with toasted coconut or your choice of toppings.

Sweet Potato Hash with Eggs

Ingredients:

- 2 medium sweet potatoes, diced
- 1/2 onion, chopped
- 1 bell pepper, chopped
- 4 eggs
- Olive oil for cooking
- Salt and pepper to taste

Instructions:

1. In a skillet, heat olive oil over medium heat. Add sweet potatoes, onion, and bell pepper. Cook until sweet potatoes are tender (about 10-12 minutes).
2. Make wells in the hash and crack an egg into each well. Cover and cook until the eggs are set.
3. Season with salt and pepper before serving.

Winter Fruit Salad with Honey

Ingredients:

- 2 apples, diced
- 2 pears, diced
- 1 cup pomegranate seeds
- 1 cup clementine segments
- 1/4 cup honey
- 1 tablespoon lemon juice
- Optional: fresh mint leaves for garnish

Instructions:

1. In a large bowl, combine diced apples, pears, pomegranate seeds, and clementine segments.
2. In a small bowl, whisk together honey and lemon juice. Pour over the fruit salad and toss gently to coat.
3. Serve immediately, garnished with fresh mint leaves if desired.

Nutty Quinoa Porridge

Ingredients:

- 1 cup quinoa, rinsed
- 2 cups almond milk (or milk of choice)
- 1/4 cup chopped nuts (almonds, walnuts, or pecans)
- 2 tablespoons maple syrup (or honey)
- 1 teaspoon vanilla extract
- Optional toppings: fresh fruit, nut butter, or additional nuts

Instructions:

1. In a saucepan, combine quinoa and almond milk. Bring to a boil, then reduce heat to low, cover, and simmer for 15-20 minutes, or until the quinoa is cooked and the milk is absorbed.
2. Stir in chopped nuts, maple syrup, and vanilla extract. Cook for an additional 2-3 minutes.
3. Serve warm, topped with your choice of toppings.

Creamy Avocado Toast with Poached Eggs

Ingredients:

- 2 slices of whole-grain bread
- 1 ripe avocado
- 2 eggs
- Salt and pepper to taste
- Optional toppings: red pepper flakes, cherry tomatoes, or fresh herbs

Instructions:

1. Toast the bread slices until golden brown.
2. In a saucepan, bring water to a simmer. Crack an egg into a small bowl, then gently slide it into the simmering water. Poach for about 3-4 minutes, or until the whites are set and the yolk is still runny. Repeat with the second egg.
3. In a bowl, mash the avocado with a fork and season with salt and pepper.
4. Spread the mashed avocado on the toasted bread, top with poached eggs, and add optional toppings as desired.

Enjoy these delicious and nutritious breakfast recipes!

Blueberry Muffin Smoothie

Ingredients:

- 1 cup frozen blueberries
- 1 banana
- 1/2 cup Greek yogurt
- 1/2 cup almond milk (or milk of choice)
- 1/2 teaspoon vanilla extract
- 1/4 teaspoon cinnamon
- Optional: oats for added texture

Instructions:

1. In a blender, combine frozen blueberries, banana, Greek yogurt, almond milk, vanilla extract, and cinnamon.
2. Blend until smooth and creamy. If desired, add oats and blend again for a thicker texture.
3. Serve immediately, garnished with fresh blueberries or a sprinkle of cinnamon.

Baked Apple Cinnamon French Toast

Ingredients:

- 6 slices of bread (French or challah)
- 2 apples, peeled and diced
- 4 eggs
- 1 cup milk
- 1/4 cup brown sugar
- 1 teaspoon vanilla extract
- 1 teaspoon ground cinnamon
- 1/4 teaspoon salt
- Optional: maple syrup for serving

Instructions:

1. Preheat the oven to 350°F (175°C). Grease a baking dish.
2. Arrange the bread slices in the baking dish. Scatter diced apples on top.
3. In a bowl, whisk together eggs, milk, brown sugar, vanilla, cinnamon, and salt. Pour the mixture over the bread and apples.
4. Bake for 30-35 minutes, or until the egg is set and the top is golden. Serve warm with maple syrup if desired.

Creamy Tomato Soup with Grilled Cheese Croutons

Ingredients:

- 2 tablespoons olive oil
- 1 onion, chopped
- 3 cloves garlic, minced
- 2 cans (14.5 oz each) diced tomatoes
- 2 cups vegetable broth
- 1/2 cup heavy cream
- Salt and pepper to taste
- Bread and cheese for croutons (your choice)

Instructions:

1. In a pot, heat olive oil over medium heat. Sauté onion and garlic until soft.
2. Add diced tomatoes and vegetable broth. Simmer for 20 minutes.
3. Blend the soup until smooth, then stir in heavy cream. Season with salt and pepper.
4. For croutons, make grilled cheese sandwiches, then cut them into small squares. Serve croutons on top of the soup.

Banana Nut Overnight Oats

Ingredients:

- 1 cup rolled oats
- 1 cup almond milk (or milk of choice)
- 1 ripe banana, mashed
- 2 tablespoons chopped nuts (walnuts or pecans)
- 1 tablespoon maple syrup (optional)
- 1/2 teaspoon vanilla extract

Instructions:

1. In a bowl, combine rolled oats, almond milk, mashed banana, nuts, maple syrup, and vanilla.
2. Stir well, cover, and refrigerate overnight.
3. In the morning, stir and enjoy cold or heated, topped with additional banana and nuts if desired.

Spiced Pear and Oatmeal Bowl

Ingredients:

- 1 cup rolled oats
- 2 cups water or milk
- 1 ripe pear, diced
- 1 teaspoon cinnamon
- 1 tablespoon maple syrup or honey
- Optional toppings: chopped nuts, dried fruit, or yogurt

Instructions:

1. In a pot, bring water or milk to a boil. Add oats, diced pear, cinnamon, and sweetener.
2. Reduce heat and simmer for about 5-7 minutes, stirring occasionally, until the oats are cooked and creamy.
3. Serve warm, topped with your choice of nuts or yogurt.

Eggnog Pancakes

Ingredients:

- 1 cup all-purpose flour
- 1 tablespoon baking powder
- 1/4 teaspoon salt
- 1 cup eggnog
- 1 large egg
- 2 tablespoons melted butter
- 1/2 teaspoon ground nutmeg

Instructions:

1. In a bowl, mix flour, baking powder, and salt. In another bowl, combine eggnog, egg, melted butter, and nutmeg.
2. Add wet ingredients to dry ingredients and stir until just combined.
3. Heat a skillet over medium heat and pour 1/4 cup batter for each pancake. Cook until bubbles form, then flip and cook until golden.
4. Serve warm with syrup or powdered sugar.

Pineapple Coconut Smoothie

Ingredients:

- 1 cup frozen pineapple chunks
- 1 banana
- 1/2 cup coconut milk (or yogurt)
- 1/2 cup almond milk (or milk of choice)
- 1 tablespoon shredded coconut (optional)

Instructions:

1. In a blender, combine frozen pineapple, banana, coconut milk, almond milk, and shredded coconut.
2. Blend until smooth and creamy. Adjust thickness with more milk if needed.
3. Serve immediately, garnished with extra shredded coconut if desired.

Enjoy these delightful recipes!

Cranberry Almond Porridge

Ingredients:

- 1 cup rolled oats
- 2 cups almond milk (or milk of choice)
- 1/4 cup dried cranberries
- 1/4 cup sliced almonds
- 2 tablespoons maple syrup or honey
- 1/2 teaspoon vanilla extract
- Pinch of salt

Instructions:

1. In a saucepan, combine rolled oats, almond milk, dried cranberries, and a pinch of salt. Bring to a boil.
2. Reduce heat and simmer for 5-7 minutes, stirring occasionally until thickened.
3. Stir in maple syrup and vanilla extract. Serve topped with sliced almonds.

Zucchini and Cheese Frittata

Ingredients:

- 4 large eggs
- 1 cup grated zucchini
- 1/2 cup shredded cheese (cheddar or feta)
- 1/4 cup milk
- Salt and pepper to taste
- 1 tablespoon olive oil

Instructions:

1. Preheat the oven to 350°F (175°C).
2. In a bowl, whisk together eggs, grated zucchini, cheese, milk, salt, and pepper.
3. In an oven-safe skillet, heat olive oil over medium heat. Pour the egg mixture into the skillet and cook for about 5 minutes until the edges set.
4. Transfer the skillet to the oven and bake for 15-20 minutes until the center is firm. Slice and serve warm.

Mushroom and Spinach Quiche

Ingredients:

- 1 pie crust (store-bought or homemade)
- 1 cup mushrooms, sliced
- 1 cup fresh spinach
- 4 large eggs
- 1 cup milk
- 1 cup shredded cheese (Swiss or cheddar)
- Salt and pepper to taste

Instructions:

1. Preheat the oven to 375°F (190°C). Line the pie crust in a pie dish.
2. In a skillet, sauté mushrooms until browned. Add spinach and cook until wilted. Spread the mixture evenly over the crust.
3. In a bowl, whisk together eggs, milk, salt, and pepper. Pour the mixture over the mushroom and spinach.
4. Sprinkle cheese on top and bake for 35-40 minutes until the quiche is set and golden. Cool slightly before slicing.

Hazelnut Chocolate Spread on Toast

Ingredients:

- 1 cup hazelnuts
- 1/4 cup cocoa powder
- 1/4 cup maple syrup or honey
- 1/2 teaspoon vanilla extract
- Pinch of salt
- Bread for toasting

Instructions:

1. Preheat the oven to 350°F (175°C) and roast hazelnuts for about 10 minutes until fragrant.
2. In a food processor, blend roasted hazelnuts until smooth. Add cocoa powder, maple syrup, vanilla, and salt. Blend until combined.
3. Toast slices of bread and spread the hazelnut chocolate mixture on top. Serve immediately.

Lemon Poppy Seed Muffins

Ingredients:

- 1 1/2 cups all-purpose flour
- 1/2 cup sugar
- 1 teaspoon baking powder
- 1/2 teaspoon baking soda
- 1/4 teaspoon salt
- 1/2 cup yogurt
- 1/4 cup vegetable oil
- 2 large eggs
- Zest of 1 lemon
- 2 tablespoons poppy seeds

Instructions:

1. Preheat the oven to 375°F (190°C). Line a muffin tin with paper liners.
2. In a bowl, whisk together flour, sugar, baking powder, baking soda, and salt. In another bowl, mix yogurt, oil, eggs, lemon zest, and poppy seeds.
3. Combine wet and dry ingredients until just mixed. Fill muffin cups about 2/3 full.
4. Bake for 18-20 minutes until a toothpick comes out clean. Allow to cool before serving.

Warm Quinoa Bowl with Apples and Cinnamon

Ingredients:

- 1 cup cooked quinoa
- 1 apple, diced
- 1/2 teaspoon cinnamon
- 1 tablespoon maple syrup (optional)
- 1/4 cup walnuts or pecans (optional)
- 1/2 cup almond milk (or milk of choice)

Instructions:

1. In a saucepan, combine cooked quinoa, diced apple, cinnamon, and almond milk. Heat over medium heat until warm.
2. Stir in maple syrup if using and cook for an additional minute.
3. Serve warm, topped with walnuts or pecans if desired.

Baked Eggs in Tomato Sauce

Ingredients:

- 1 can (14 oz) diced tomatoes
- 4 large eggs
- 2 cloves garlic, minced
- 1/2 teaspoon paprika
- Salt and pepper to taste
- Fresh basil or parsley for garnish
- Olive oil for drizzling

Instructions:

1. Preheat the oven to 375°F (190°C). In a baking dish, combine diced tomatoes, garlic, paprika, salt, and pepper.
2. Make small wells in the tomato mixture and crack an egg into each well.
3. Drizzle with olive oil and bake for 15-20 minutes until eggs are set to your liking. Garnish with fresh herbs before serving.

Enjoy these delicious recipes!

Cocoa Oatmeal with Banana

Ingredients:

- 1 cup rolled oats
- 2 cups milk (or water)
- 2 tablespoons unsweetened cocoa powder
- 1 tablespoon maple syrup (or honey)
- 1 banana, sliced
- Pinch of salt
- Optional toppings: nuts, chocolate chips, or additional banana slices

Instructions:

1. In a saucepan, combine rolled oats, milk (or water), cocoa powder, and salt. Bring to a boil.
2. Reduce heat and simmer for 5-7 minutes, stirring occasionally, until the oatmeal thickens.
3. Stir in maple syrup and top with banana slices and any additional toppings before serving.

Honey Almond Butter Toast

Ingredients:

- 2 slices whole-grain bread
- 2 tablespoons almond butter
- 1 tablespoon honey
- Sliced banana or berries (optional)
- Chia seeds or crushed nuts (optional)

Instructions:

1. Toast the slices of bread until golden brown.
2. Spread almond butter evenly on each slice of toast.
3. Drizzle with honey and top with sliced banana or berries, if desired. Sprinkle chia seeds or crushed nuts for added texture.

Sourdough Bread Pudding

Ingredients:

- 4 cups cubed sourdough bread
- 2 cups milk
- 4 large eggs
- 1/2 cup sugar
- 1 teaspoon vanilla extract
- 1 teaspoon ground cinnamon
- Optional: raisins or chocolate chips

Instructions:

1. Preheat the oven to 350°F (175°C). Grease a baking dish.
2. In a large bowl, whisk together milk, eggs, sugar, vanilla, and cinnamon.
3. Add cubed sourdough bread and stir to combine. Let it sit for 10-15 minutes to soak.
4. If desired, stir in raisins or chocolate chips. Pour the mixture into the prepared baking dish.
5. Bake for 30-35 minutes until set and golden brown. Let cool slightly before serving.

Maple Syrup Sweet Potato Pancakes

Ingredients:

- 1 cup mashed sweet potatoes (cooked)
- 1 cup all-purpose flour
- 1 tablespoon baking powder
- 1/2 teaspoon salt
- 1/2 teaspoon cinnamon
- 1 cup milk
- 1 large egg
- 2 tablespoons maple syrup
- Butter or oil for cooking

Instructions:

1. In a bowl, mix together mashed sweet potatoes, flour, baking powder, salt, and cinnamon.
2. In another bowl, whisk together milk, egg, and maple syrup. Combine wet and dry ingredients until just mixed.
3. Heat a skillet over medium heat and add butter or oil. Pour batter onto the skillet and cook until bubbles form on the surface. Flip and cook until golden brown.
4. Serve with additional maple syrup.

Warm Cinnamon Apples with Yogurt

Ingredients:

- 2 apples, peeled, cored, and diced
- 1 teaspoon cinnamon
- 1 tablespoon maple syrup or honey
- 1 tablespoon butter
- Greek yogurt for serving

Instructions:

1. In a skillet, melt butter over medium heat. Add diced apples and sprinkle with cinnamon and maple syrup.
2. Cook for 5-7 minutes, stirring occasionally, until apples are tender.
3. Serve warm over a dollop of Greek yogurt.

Savory Oatmeal with Mushrooms and Cheese

Ingredients:

- 1 cup rolled oats
- 2 cups vegetable broth or water
- 1 cup mushrooms, sliced
- 1/2 cup shredded cheese (cheddar or your choice)
- 1 tablespoon olive oil
- Salt and pepper to taste
- Optional toppings: chopped herbs or a fried egg

Instructions:

1. In a saucepan, bring vegetable broth or water to a boil. Add rolled oats and cook according to package instructions.
2. In a skillet, heat olive oil over medium heat. Sauté mushrooms until browned and tender. Season with salt and pepper.
3. Once the oats are cooked, stir in shredded cheese until melted. Serve topped with sautéed mushrooms and optional toppings.

Homemade Breakfast Burritos

Ingredients:

- 4 large tortillas
- 4 large eggs
- 1/2 cup cooked and crumbled sausage or cooked veggies
- 1/2 cup shredded cheese
- 1/4 cup salsa
- Salt and pepper to taste
- Optional toppings: avocado, sour cream, or cilantro

Instructions:

1. In a bowl, whisk eggs with salt and pepper. Scramble eggs in a skillet until fully cooked.
2. Lay tortillas flat and layer scrambled eggs, sausage (or veggies), cheese, and salsa in the center.
3. Roll up the tortillas tightly, folding in the sides. Heat in a skillet until golden and warm.
4. Serve with optional toppings.

Enjoy these delightful breakfast recipes!

Creamy Polenta with Sausage and Egg

Ingredients:

- 1 cup polenta
- 4 cups water or broth
- 1 cup grated Parmesan cheese
- 1 pound sausage (Italian or your choice)
- 4 eggs
- Salt and pepper to taste
- Fresh herbs for garnish (optional)

Instructions:

1. In a large saucepan, bring water or broth to a boil. Gradually whisk in the polenta. Reduce heat and simmer, stirring frequently, until thickened (about 15-20 minutes).
2. Stir in Parmesan cheese, salt, and pepper. Keep warm.
3. In a skillet, cook the sausage over medium heat until browned and cooked through. Remove and keep warm.
4. In the same skillet, fry the eggs to your liking (sunny side up or over easy).
5. To serve, spoon creamy polenta into bowls, top with sausage and an egg, and garnish with fresh herbs if desired.

Chocolate Chip Banana Bread

Ingredients:

- 3 ripe bananas, mashed
- 1/3 cup melted butter
- 1 teaspoon baking soda
- Pinch of salt
- 3/4 cup sugar
- 1 large egg, beaten
- 1 teaspoon vanilla extract
- 1 cup all-purpose flour
- 1/2 cup chocolate chips

Instructions:

1. Preheat the oven to 350°F (175°C). Grease a 9x5-inch loaf pan.
2. In a mixing bowl, mix mashed bananas with melted butter. Stir in baking soda and salt.
3. Add sugar, beaten egg, and vanilla extract. Mix well.
4. Stir in flour and fold in chocolate chips until just combined.
5. Pour the batter into the prepared loaf pan and bake for 60-65 minutes, or until a toothpick comes out clean. Let cool before slicing.

Strawberry and Cream Cheese Stuffed French Toast

Ingredients:

- 4 slices thick bread (such as challah or brioche)
- 4 ounces cream cheese, softened
- 1 cup fresh strawberries, sliced
- 2 large eggs
- 1/2 cup milk
- 1 teaspoon vanilla extract
- Butter for cooking
- Powdered sugar for serving (optional)

Instructions:

1. Spread cream cheese on two slices of bread, and layer with sliced strawberries. Top with the remaining bread to create sandwiches.
2. In a bowl, whisk together eggs, milk, and vanilla extract. Dip each sandwich in the egg mixture, coating both sides.
3. In a skillet, melt butter over medium heat. Cook the sandwiches until golden brown on both sides, about 3-4 minutes per side.
4. Serve warm, dusted with powdered sugar if desired.

Spicy Sausage and Egg Breakfast Wrap

Ingredients:

- 4 large tortillas
- 1 pound spicy sausage, crumbled
- 4 large eggs
- 1/2 cup shredded cheese (cheddar or your choice)
- 1/4 cup salsa
- Avocado slices (optional)
- Salt and pepper to taste

Instructions:

1. In a skillet, cook crumbled sausage over medium heat until browned. Remove and keep warm.
2. In the same skillet, scramble eggs with salt and pepper until cooked through.
3. To assemble, lay a tortilla flat and layer with sausage, scrambled eggs, cheese, and salsa. Add avocado slices if desired.
4. Roll up the tortilla tightly and serve warm.

Butternut Squash Soup with Toasted Seeds

Ingredients:

- 1 medium butternut squash, peeled and diced
- 1 onion, chopped
- 2 cloves garlic, minced
- 4 cups vegetable broth
- 1 teaspoon ground cumin
- Salt and pepper to taste
- Pumpkin or sunflower seeds for garnish
- Olive oil for drizzling

Instructions:

1. In a large pot, heat olive oil over medium heat. Add onion and garlic; sauté until softened.
2. Add diced butternut squash, vegetable broth, cumin, salt, and pepper. Bring to a boil, then reduce heat and simmer until squash is tender (about 20-25 minutes).
3. Use an immersion blender to puree the soup until smooth. Adjust seasoning as needed.
4. Serve warm, garnished with toasted seeds and a drizzle of olive oil.

Cinnamon Sugar Donuts

Ingredients:

- 1 cup all-purpose flour
- 1/2 cup sugar
- 1 teaspoon baking powder
- 1/2 teaspoon cinnamon
- 1/4 teaspoon salt
- 1/2 cup milk
- 1/4 cup melted butter
- 1 large egg
- 1/2 cup sugar mixed with 1 teaspoon cinnamon (for coating)

Instructions:

1. Preheat the oven to 350°F (175°C) and grease a donut pan.
2. In a mixing bowl, combine flour, sugar, baking powder, cinnamon, and salt. In another bowl, mix milk, melted butter, and egg.
3. Combine wet and dry ingredients until just mixed. Fill the donut pan about halfway with batter.
4. Bake for 10-12 minutes, or until golden brown. Let cool slightly before removing from the pan.
5. Roll warm donuts in cinnamon sugar to coat.

Rice Pudding with Cardamom

Ingredients:

- 1 cup cooked rice
- 2 cups milk
- 1/2 cup sugar
- 1 teaspoon ground cardamom
- 1 teaspoon vanilla extract
- 1/4 cup raisins or dried fruit (optional)
- Ground cinnamon for serving (optional)

Instructions:

1. In a saucepan, combine cooked rice, milk, sugar, cardamom, and vanilla. Cook over medium heat until heated through.
2. Stir in raisins or dried fruit if using. Continue cooking until the mixture thickens (about 10-15 minutes).
3. Serve warm, sprinkled with ground cinnamon if desired.

Enjoy these delicious recipes!

Berry Smoothie Bowl with Granola

Ingredients:

- 1 cup mixed berries (fresh or frozen)
- 1 banana
- 1/2 cup Greek yogurt
- 1/2 cup almond milk (or any milk of choice)
- 1 tablespoon honey or maple syrup (optional)
- Granola for topping
- Fresh berries and nuts for garnish (optional)

Instructions:

1. In a blender, combine mixed berries, banana, Greek yogurt, almond milk, and honey or maple syrup. Blend until smooth.
2. Pour the smoothie mixture into a bowl and top with granola, fresh berries, and nuts if desired.
3. Serve immediately and enjoy!

Oven-Baked Omelet with Veggies

Ingredients:

- 6 large eggs
- 1/2 cup milk
- 1 cup diced vegetables (bell peppers, onions, spinach, etc.)
- 1 cup shredded cheese (cheddar, feta, or your choice)
- Salt and pepper to taste
- Fresh herbs for garnish (optional)

Instructions:

1. Preheat the oven to 350°F (175°C) and grease a baking dish.
2. In a bowl, whisk together eggs and milk. Season with salt and pepper.
3. Stir in diced vegetables and cheese. Pour the mixture into the prepared baking dish.
4. Bake for 25-30 minutes, or until the omelet is set and lightly golden. Let cool for a few minutes, then slice and serve garnished with fresh herbs if desired.

Baked Oatmeal with Apples and Raisins

Ingredients:

- 2 cups rolled oats
- 1/2 cup brown sugar
- 1 teaspoon baking powder
- 1 teaspoon cinnamon
- 1/2 teaspoon salt
- 2 cups milk
- 2 large eggs
- 2 apples, diced
- 1/2 cup raisins
- 1 teaspoon vanilla extract

Instructions:

1. Preheat the oven to 350°F (175°C) and grease a baking dish.
2. In a large bowl, mix oats, brown sugar, baking powder, cinnamon, and salt.
3. In another bowl, whisk together milk, eggs, apples, raisins, and vanilla extract.
4. Combine wet and dry ingredients and pour into the prepared baking dish. Bake for 30-35 minutes, until set. Serve warm.

Chocolate Hazelnut Overnight Oats

Ingredients:

- 1 cup rolled oats
- 1 cup milk (or non-dairy alternative)
- 2 tablespoons chocolate hazelnut spread
- 1 tablespoon chia seeds (optional)
- 1 tablespoon maple syrup (optional)
- Fresh fruit and nuts for topping

Instructions:

1. In a jar or container, combine rolled oats, milk, chocolate hazelnut spread, chia seeds, and maple syrup. Stir well to combine.
2. Cover and refrigerate overnight (or for at least 4 hours).
3. In the morning, stir the oats and top with fresh fruit and nuts before serving.

Savory Breakfast Polenta

Ingredients:

- 1 cup polenta
- 4 cups water or broth
- 1 cup grated cheese (Parmesan or your choice)
- 1 cup cooked vegetables (spinach, mushrooms, etc.)
- 2 poached eggs (optional)
- Salt and pepper to taste

Instructions:

1. In a saucepan, bring water or broth to a boil. Gradually whisk in polenta. Reduce heat and cook, stirring frequently, until thickened (about 15-20 minutes).
2. Stir in grated cheese, salt, and pepper. Serve topped with cooked vegetables and a poached egg if desired.

Ricotta and Berry Toast

Ingredients:

- 4 slices of bread (whole grain or your choice)
- 1 cup ricotta cheese
- 1 cup mixed berries (strawberries, blueberries, raspberries)
- Honey for drizzling
- Fresh mint for garnish (optional)

Instructions:

1. Toast the bread slices until golden brown.
2. Spread a generous layer of ricotta cheese on each slice of toast.
3. Top with mixed berries and drizzle with honey. Garnish with fresh mint if desired.

Cinnamon Apple Pancakes

Ingredients:

- 1 cup all-purpose flour
- 1 tablespoon baking powder
- 1 teaspoon cinnamon
- 1/4 teaspoon salt
- 1 cup milk
- 1 large egg
- 1 tablespoon melted butter
- 1 apple, grated
- Maple syrup for serving

Instructions:

1. In a mixing bowl, combine flour, baking powder, cinnamon, and salt.
2. In another bowl, whisk together milk, egg, and melted butter. Stir in grated apple.
3. Combine wet and dry ingredients until just mixed.
4. Heat a skillet over medium heat and pour batter onto the skillet to form pancakes. Cook until bubbles form on the surface, then flip and cook until golden brown. Serve with maple syrup.

Winter Root Vegetable Hash

Ingredients:

- 2 cups mixed root vegetables (sweet potatoes, carrots, parsnips, etc.), diced
- 1 onion, chopped
- 2 tablespoons olive oil
- 2 cloves garlic, minced
- 4 large eggs
- Salt and pepper to taste
- Fresh herbs for garnish (optional)

Instructions:

1. In a large skillet, heat olive oil over medium heat. Add diced root vegetables and onion, cooking until softened and lightly browned (about 15-20 minutes).
2. Stir in garlic and cook for another minute. Season with salt and pepper.
3. Create wells in the hash and crack an egg into each well. Cover the skillet and cook until eggs are set to your liking.
4. Serve warm, garnished with fresh herbs if desired.

Enjoy these delicious breakfast recipes!

www.ingramcontent.com/pod-product-compliance
Lightning Source LLC
LaVergne TN
LVHW081334060526
838201LV00055B/2638